TILT

SIX TALES

EDITED BY
EVE GREENWOOD AND HARI CONNER

BOOK DESIGN BY
EVE GREENWOOD

COVER ART BY
FRAN MORTON

TABLE OF CONTENTS

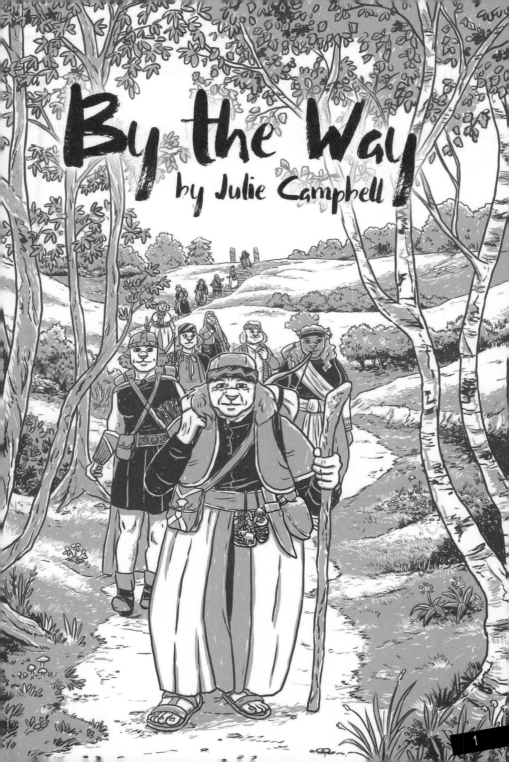

By the Way
by Julie Campbell

HUFF

YOU'RE A CAPTAIN AT DEGOLA, THEN?

HERE I THOUGHT I WAS TRAVELLING CASUAL-LIKE.

YOUR CAPTAIN'S STAR IS STILL PINNED TO YOUR CLOAK.

THAT IT IS.

AYE, I'VE BEEN A CAPTAIN THERE THREE FULL YEARS. MOVED THERE FROM CAMSHORT.

YOU TRAINED AT FORT GARNSHAW AT CAMSHORT? HAD A FRIEND WENT THAT ROUTE LONG AGO.

SERVED MY TIME THERE, YES. LIKED CAMSHORT A LOT, GREAT PLACE FOR YOUNGSTERS TO GET IN TROUBLE AFTER A FULL DAY'S TRAINING! THE FESTIVALS, THE PARADES...

I USED TO VISIT FOR THOSE PARADES WITH MY FAMILY WHEN I WAS LITTLE, THEY WERE SO—

OH! I NEARLY FORGOT, THERE'S A WONDERFUL VIEW, NETHAN. WE WOULD ALWAYS STOP JUST HERE FOR A LITTLE FOOD AND A BREAK. MORDENNA ALWAYS SAID...

WELL. IT'S WORTH STOPPING FOR.

NICE VIEW AND A GOOD TIME FOR A BITE, LIKE YOU SAY.

DO YOU LIKE IT? THE WARRIOR LIFE?

I DO. IT HAS ITS UPS AND DOWNS, RIGHT ENOUGH.

I'VE LOST FIGHTS, LOST PEOPLE. BUT I'VE TRAVELLED, SURVIVED BATTLES, SEEN PLACES.

PROTECTING THOSE LESS ABLE SEEMS WORTH IT.

RATHER FANCIED THE WARRIOR LIFE MYSELF AT ONE TIME, BACK WHEN I WAS YOUNG, STRONG AND BRAVE.

IT'S BEEN A LONG TIME, BUT I WAS A TOWN GUARD BACK IN CALYFORT. MANY YEARS AGO, IN MY YOUTH.

MANY BORDER SKIRMISHES THEN, BACK BEFORE THE PEACE WAS BROKERED. BUSY TIME, DANGEROUS TOO. BUT I LOVED IT.

NOTICED YOUR FORM BACK WHEN THAT POSKA WAS GIVING TROUBLE, I DID.

THOUGHT TO MYSELF, HERE'S A LADY THAT CAN LOOK AFTER HERSELF!

BEST SHOT IN THE PARISH, I WAS.

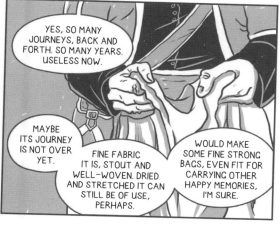

MORNING! HOPE YOU MANAGED SOME SLEEP. THE RAINS LOOK TO BE HOLDING OFF FOR NOW, SO WE'RE MAKING READY TO MOVE.

NONSENSE. YESTERDAY WAS A TOUGH DAY, YOU NEEDED THE SLEEP.

I'M PARRY, BY THE WAY.

NETHAN HAS TOLD ME ALL ABOUT YOUR JOURNEY. YOU'RE HEADED FOR HELMSFORD?

YES, OF COURSE.

OH, IT'S SO LATE, YOU COULD HAVE WOKEN ME EARLIER.

I'M MOVING THERE.

I FARMED IN CALYFORT BUT MY WIFE DIED A FEW YEARS BACK.

I CARRIED ON, BUT IT'S TOO MUCH FOR ME NOW. I'M GOING TO LIVE WITH MY DAUGHTER'S FAMILY.

SO THE START OF A NEW ADVENTURE THEN.

SUCH A LOVELY VIEW! A MUDDY ONE AFTER LAST NIGHT'S RAINS, BUT LOVELY TO BE SURE.

I'VE SEEN THIS VIEW IN SUN, RAIN AND SNOW.

MAYBE A NEW DRAWING FOR YOUR TENT? IS IT PAINTING YOU MOSTLY DO?

STORY PAINTING MOSTLY, AND I TEACH AT LOCHAN COLLEGE.

ON TO VISIT THE BIG GALLERIES IN MUSTO NOW, TO SEE THE ART.

THERE WAS A WOOD-CARVING TEACHER AT LOCHAN, MES EMBO.

WAS TAUGHT BY HIM A LITTLE, WHEN HE TRAVELLED.

OH, HE WAS A MASTER. AN HONOUR TO BE TAUGHT BY HIM. YOU DIDN'T PURSUE YOUR CARVING?

NO, FARMING WAS MY LIFE, BUT I LEARNED MUCH FROM HIM.

ALWAYS WONDERED IF I COULD HAVE BEEN A CARVER, BUT I STILL CARVED WHEN I HAD THE TIME.

TOMIN SOMETIMES, OR CARVED HEADPOSTS OR FENCES. CARVING FOR THE LITTLE ONES, THAT SORT OF THING.

CAREFUL NOW, PATH GETS NARROW HERE AND THERE'S SOME SLIPPAGE.

OOF, WISH I'D NOT BROUGHT SO MANY SUPPLIES. YOU TRAVEL LIGHT, HETTA, FOR ONE MOVING.

MOST OF WHAT I HAD WAS FOR THE FARM, BEST LEFT TO THE NICE FAMILY TAKING IT ON.

THINGS ARE ONLY THINGS, AFTER ALL.

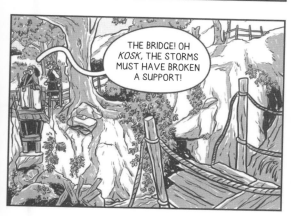

THE BRIDGE! OH KOSK, THE STORMS MUST HAVE BROKEN A SUPPORT!

NO OTHER CROSSING POINTS?

NO, THIS IS THE ONLY ONE. THE OTHER WAY ROUND TAKES WEEKS.

WE MUST CROSS.

HOW?

THE END SEEMS SOLID. IT'S THE MIDDLE PLANKS THAT HAVE GONE. I DON'T FANCY THE JUMP.

NETHAN, COULD YOU FIRE AN ARROW WITH A LINE ATTACHED OVER THAT TREE BRANCH?

19

WELL, HERE WE ARE.

LEFT LEADS TO DEGOLA, RIGHT TO MUSTO, ONWARDS TO HELMSFORD FOR ME.

THIS IS WHERE WE WOULD SAY GOODBYE, I THINK.

IF YOU WERE REAL, THAT IS.

I SUPPOSE YOU'VE BOTH ALREADY HAD YOUR SAY THOUGH, HAVEN'T YOU?

THANK YOU, MY IMAGINED ROAD COMPANIONS. YOU GAVE ME SOMEONE TO TALK TO ON MY LONELY WAY.

GAVE ME COURAGE AND HEART WHEN I MOST NEEDED IT.

I GUESS I CONJURED YOU UP AS LIVES I MIGHT ONCE HAVE LED, PATHS I DIDN'T TAKE.

ME ALL SAD AND THINKING BACK ON MY LIFE, LOOKING FOR REGRETS AND MISTAKES.

End.

Gastrotelepathy

BY
JACK DEVEREAUX

FRESH PORK GYOZA!

HOT DAMN!

UP NEXT, MAC & CHEESE WITH A CHEESE AND CRUMB CRUST!

IT SAYS MAC & CHEESE!

WHAT, N-NO, THAT'S NOT—

CAUGHT LYING, YOU'RE PAYING TRIPLE!

31

32

I THOUGHT THIS WAS A RESTAURANT, NOT A CARNIVAL. I'M OUT OF HERE.

(MUGU) MUNCH

(MUGU) MUNCH

(KIN KON) DING DONG

WELCOME SIR, PLEASE COME IN!

CAN I TAKE YOUR BAGS?

WHA— DID SHE TELEPORT HERE?!

HANDS OFF! I'LL KEEP THEM WITH ME, THANK YOU VERY MUCH.

WHAT THE—

NOW THEN, TELL ME...

WHAT DOES YOUR STOMACH DESIRE?

33

39

HUH?!

WHAT ARE YOU TALKING ABOUT?

IT'S HARD TO PUT INTO WORDS.

IT'S LIKE DEJA VU. YOU FEEL LIKE YOU'VE LIVED THIS BEFORE, BUT SOMETHING FEELS OFF.

HOW DID YOU GET YOUR HANDS ON THOSE KING TRUFFLES THE ROOST USES?

OH, I DIDN'T! THEY COST MORE THAN T BUILDING!

I JUST BLENDED SOME GARLIC, PHENOL AND MUSHROOMS INTO A PASTE TO SIMULATE THE TASTE OF TRUFFLES.

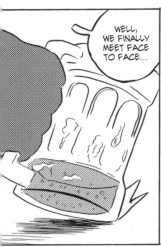

WELL, WE FINALLY MEET FACE TO FACE...

GOLDEN GLOVE.

YOU KNOW, FOR SUCH A FAMOUS UP-AND-COMING THIEF, YOU SURE FELL FOR OUR TRAP EASILY...

CLOSING DOWN THE TRUFFLE ROOST,

LEADING YOU HERE, AND GOADING YOU INTO LETTING YOUR DEFENSES DOWN.

IT WAS A NICE PLAN, DETECTIVE.

42

LOOK FOR THE SMELL OF SAKE OR NUTTY SHIITAKE.

SAKE, HE'S CLEAR.

EASY ONE, DAIRY BREATH. I USED HEAVY CREAM AND FOUR CHEESES.

OOF, YEAH, DAIRY. SHE'S CLEAR.

OH GOD OH GOD

THE SHALLOTS AND LEMONGRASS SHOULD BE EASY TO CATCH.

47

49

I'LL GET EVEN WITH YOU, YOU SORRY EXCUSE FOR A CHEF!

YOU'VE DEFILED MY TASTEBUDS!

YOU THINK YOUR JAIL CAN HOLD ME?!

I'LL BE GONE BEFORE YOU GET BACK TO THE STATION!

I WILL DINE ON THE KING'S TRUFFLES AGAIN!

パタン (PATAN) (SLAM)

(GO GO GO) RUMBLE

(PIKU) FLINCH

OKAY, HOW ABOUT A ROUND OF BAR SNACKS FOR EVERYONE?

ピーポー (PI~ PO~) (WEE~ WOO~)

ピーポー (PI~ PO~) (WEE~ WOO~)

POLICE

WOO!

(YEAH, I COULD EAT.)

ALL RIGHT!

50

WHAT HAVE WE LEARNED? NEVER INSULT A CHEF'S COOKING!

THE END

In Lilac and Silver

by Cara Gaffney

In Loving Memory

Arina Gray

18 DECEMBER 2022 - 1 MAY 2109

Beloved Sister, Aunt, and Friend

14th May 2109
1pm
Dunforar Conservatory

DING-DONG
DING-DONG

I'm over here.

You look tired.

Well...

I did bury my sister yesterday.

So you spoke to the android people after all...

Yes.

All my memories, all my ways of thinking.

They're all in this body now.

I know the idea behind these models is to step into the shoes of the one who passed away.

But you weren't expecting this, so I want you to know--

--I'm not going to insert myself into your life if you don't want that.

I can--

N-no, I--

Rini--

This was a last-minute decision, and... It wasn't really about them.

You didn't need to do this. You always said you didn't believe...

It wasn't about what I believe. I mean—

I did think death would be the end of me. That who I was - my 'self' - could only be *copied* into a new body, not *transferred*. But you thought differently, and...

...well, I didn't want you to be lonely.

It was a little selfish, I know.

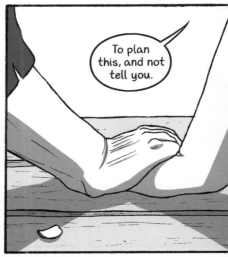
To plan this, and not tell you.

But I thought...

If I were going to die, I wanted my last days to be about *me*.

Not about... whatever followed.

What... do you think now?

That's a funny question to ask, right?

Do I believe I'm the same 'Arina'?

If I say "Yes, I changed my mind, I'm the original after all"--

--does that *prove* I'm a copy?

Or that I really *did* just change my mind--

Rini.

Sorry!

I'm alive.

And I have the same memories.

There's nothing inauthentic about how I'm acting, is there?

But do I believe I'm 'her'...

No, I suppose I don't.

Her perfect twin, maybe.

Which is a funny way to put it...

I used to love when people thought we were twins.

Same.

All those matching dresses when we were kids.

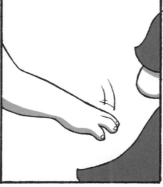

The dress you're wearing now is - really nice.

You look...

They did a very good job.

Haha, thank you!

They kept on reminding me I could make myself look however I wanted--

--but I put so much work into accepting myself over the years!

And my forties were great.

(haha) That's the most un-Rini thing you've said so far.

Wait, what?

The menopause?

God! You're right, I take it back.

Forgetting your human problems already...

Truly. I should have done this robot thing years ago.

I've missed this.

I've missed you, so much.

It's only been a week, but every day I wake up and wonder why--

--why everything is still going.

Don't they know how wrong the world is?

Don't they know that you died?

But... to continue on, as things were before...

Isn't that what wanted?

I hope I'm not being unfair to you.

No, not at all.

It's funny...

Even after all these years, I wasn't sure what you would do.

I thought you'd prefer having 'me' here...

But this choice makes me happy, too.

Love you, Rini.

Love you too.

Seven years later...

I didn't want you to be lonely, either.

PROVIDENCE!

by Chris Manson

THIS IS **BULLSHIT** MAN!

HOW THE HELL DO WE GOTTA RE-APPLY FOR OUR JOBS? I BEEN HERE FOUR YEARS!

YEAH, WHO DO VILLASPACE THINK THEY ARE?

NEW MANAGEMENT WANTS TO RETOOL THE PLACE, THEY NEED FOLKS WITH DIFFERENT SKILLS, I GUESS.

LOOK, WE... WE TRIED. I'M SORRY. I'M IN THE SAME BOAT, Y'KNOW?

TRACE... YOU'RE BAYSIDE'S COUNCILLOR. CAN'T YOU FIGHT 'EM THERE?

WE NEED THESE JOBS, MA YOU KNOW IT.

I'M SORRY, FEE. WE JUST DON'T HAVE THE RESOURCES.

COMPANIES LIKE VILLASPACE, THEY... THEY CAN AFFORD ACCOUNTANTS AND LAWYERS, AND THEIR PROBLEMS JUST EVAPORATE.

EVERYONE, GO HOME. TRY TO GE SOME SLEEP, 'KAY?

F. HILL

VILLASPACE REALTY

[RESIDENT_NAME], CONGRATULATIONS!

Dear [RESIDENT_NAME], This building is now managed by Villaspace Developments. We're thrilled to have you as part of our family! Exciting new amenities are already being ~~ed~~ for your neighbourhood, and your monthly contribution will be adjusted upwards by 10% starting from today. If you are unable to meet this target, please contact your new Resident Services representative on [VL_PROP_RN] who will happily help you plan your exit.

≠CTH...≠

YO, FEE...

...YOU OKAY?

ELLE...

CRUMPH

≠SOB≠

=SNRR= MMPH... WHAT... WH[AT] TIME IS IT.

I ALWAYS FORGET HOW BIG YOUR PLACE IS...

EH, IT'S MY DAD'S, REALLY. I'M JUST BORROWING IT WHILE HE'S OUTTA TOWN.

DIDN'T WAKE YOU, DID I?

NAH. FIGURED I'D BE THE ONE NOT SLEEPING, THOUGH.

THANKS FOR LETTING ME CRASH.

NEVER FACE A CRISIS ALONE.

SOMETHING BUGGED ME ABOUT THAT COMPANY, VILLASPACE. I KEEP SEEING THEIR NAME EVERYWHERE.

THEY'VE ONLY EXISTED FOR ABOUT A YEAR, AND NONE OF THE BOARD HAVE ANY PREVIOUS BUSINESS EXPERIENCE OR HISTORY.

BUT THEY HAVE A DOZEN NEW PROJECTS HERE IN THE LAST SIX MONTHS ALONE...

I BROKE INTO T[HE] FINANCE CLOUD [TO] FIGURE OUT HOW [THE] HELL A COMPAN[Y] LIKE THAT GET[S] FUNDING.

02:37

VILLASPACE REALTY

D IT. GETS. WEIRD.

MOST OF THE DETAILS ARE ENCRYPTED, BUT FUNDING GETS DRIP-FED INTO VILLASPACE FROM A BUNCH OF OTHER, BIGGER ACCOUNTS.

AND EVERY TIME A PAYMENT'S MADE, THIS ONE AT THE BOTTOM TAKES A PERCENT.

HERE'S A AM GOING N HERE.

AND I WANNA NOW WHO'S BEHIND IT.

HOW WE GONNA DO THAT?

CAN'T DO IT FROM HERE. WE HAVE TO ACCESS THE FINANCIAL NETWORK DIRECTLY.

WE'RE GOING TO THE TRANSIT NEXUS.

85

WHAT THE HELL IS THIS PLACE?

BELLY OF THE BEAST. ALL FINANCIAL TRANSACTIONS IN CASH CITY ARE HANDLED BY THE AI CLUSTER HERE.

FINANCIAL ADVICE! FIRST ONE'S FREE!

THERE. WE NEED TO GRAB ONE OF THOSE PRIVATE BOOTHS.

COURTESY BOOTH

HEY!

WHAM!

OOPS! SORRY, MAN. CLUMSY!

NYEHEHE

ALLLLLLRIGHT.

AAAND... HERE WE

KLIP

86

SO, UH, WHAT RE WE DOING HERE?

DECRYPTING THE ACCOUNT DATA USING A KEY.

I... MIGHT HAVE STOLEN IT FROM SOME CREEPY BUSINESS DUDE IN A BAR.

LEARNED BOTH TRICKS FROM MY DAD.

GIMME A SEC HERE...

P BIP BIP

■□■■■■5

PING!

1OFOOF5

MERGING AND UPDATING... FIX THE CHECK BYTE...

HUH. THAT'S WEIRD.

SO, THIS GUY NG PAID OUT OF VILLASPACE?

nalsall Holdings Prov

- Bayside Providence Pr

- FastCash East Provide

- Providence Unity

- PROV - GRO

HE'S "BIG GEE", AN ALLEGED LOCAL ENTREPRENEUR.

VillaSpace Realty

Gee McD

Blue Water Consolidated Account

BUT THESE OTHER ACCOUNTS...?

WHY WOULD PROVIDENT FUNDS –

PENSIONS –

INVEST IN SOMETHING AS RISKY AS A CONSTRUCTION STARTUP?

AND WHAT'S BIG GEE'S INVOLVEMENT IN ALL THIS...?

SHFFT

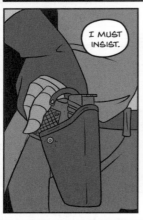

HEY, BACK OFF!

THE HELL YOU TALKING ABOUT, "THE BIZ"?

I'M JUST TRYNA FIND THE GUYS WHO TOOK MY JOB, MAN!

PLEHH

FEIGNING IGNORANCE WON'T PROTECT YOU.

ONE WORD FROM ME, ONE SCRA OF EVIDENCE, A PROVIDENCE WO TURN EVERYTHI OVER TO ME IN INSTANT!

YOU AND I BOTH KNOW THAT THEY EXPECT RESULTS. NOT BACKSTABBING AND POWER GRABS.

...PROVIDENCE. NOW I GET IT.

HEH. BIG TALK, BIG GEE. BUT YOU'RE RIGHT.

PROVIDENCE *SHOULD* COME FIRST.

SO HOW D'YOU THINK THEY'D DEAL WITH SOMEBODY STEALING FROM THEM?

ONE SCRAP OF EVIDENCE FROM ME ABOUT YOUR LITTLE SKIMMING OPERATION...

AND THEY WOU TAKE IT A FROM YOU

≋HNFH!≋

RRRAGH!

WHOA, WHOA!

KRAKK

JUST TAKE A MINUTE, BOSS.

C'MON. CLEAR YOUR HEAD.

ASSHOLE! YOU UNTIE ME, THEN WE'LL SEE!

ELLE, YOU OKAY?

BIG GEE...

WHAT AN IDIOT!

EVERYTHING MAKES SENSE NOW.

OW DOES ANY F THIS MAKE ENSE TO YOU?

WHO DOES THIS DUDE THINK WE WORK FOR?

SO, THOSE ACCOUNTS I FOUND - I MISREAD THEM. THEY'RE NOT "PROVIDENT FUNDS".

THEY BELONG TO AN ORGANISATION CALLING ITSELF "PROVIDENCE".

HE WORKS FOR THEM, AND THINKS WE DO TOO.

WAIT, HOW DID YOU GET OUT THOSE TIES...?

ANOTHER TRICK FROM MY DAD.

LET ME GET YOURS, TOO...

SO... WHY IS BIG GEE MAD AT YOU?

GOT MAD WHEN MENTIONED HIS RSONAL ACCOUNT, ONFIRMING WHAT I SUSPECTED.

HE STEALS A LITTLE EXTRA FOR HIMSELF EVERY TIME HE SENDS THEM THEIR PROFITS.

AND THEY'RE POWERFUL ENOUGH THAT HE'S SCARED OF THEM FINDING OUT.

THIS ISN'T JUST A SCAM. THERE'S A MUCH BIGGER CONSPIRACY HERE.

AND THAT DUMBASS WANNABE-BILLIONAIRE IS GONNA HELP US FIND OUT MORE.

LISTEN UP...

BRB, OFF TO TELL PROVIDENCE ABOUT YOUR SKIMMING FUND BYEEEE :) X

THOSE F—

X. CAR. NOW.

WHERE—?

THE PYRAMID WE NEED TO G[ ] THERE BEFOR[ ] THEY DO!

GO!

SKREEEEK!

VRMMMMM

THE PYRAMID, HUH?

SCREEEEECH!

WHERE ARE THEY...?

DID WE GET HERE FIRST...?

BEEP BEEP!

'SUP, LOSERS?

K! SHOVE 'EM IN THE CAR, WE'RE GETTING THEM OUT OF HERE!

REALLY? YOU WANNA MAKE A SCENE?

RIGHT OUTSIDE PROVIDENCE?

NOW HOW DO I GET IN HERE...?

EEP

VRRRT!

HAH! YOU **WISH!**

IT'LL NEVER HAPPEN!

EVEN LOYAL SOLDIERS LIKE ME NEVER SET FOOT IN THERE!

GREETINGS.

'SUP.

Elle Chong YunNgiuk
張雲玉
2038-08-08
151cm

Known Affiliations:
Cash City Alumni
WatPharm Loyalty Club
ArtMarker Monthly
黑蓮

Fiona Tamara Hill
2038-08-07
183cm

Known Affiliations:
Bayside Burger Shac
Bayside Library
Bail Autho

ELLE CHONG. YOUNGEST DAUGHTER OF ANTHONY CHONG.

WE HAVE BEEN TRYING TO CONTACT YOUR ORGANISATION FOR SOME TIME.

?

NO KIDDING, HUH?

ARE YOU HERE TO NEGOTIATE ON BEHALF OF THE BLACK LOTUS?

EEEEEEH. SURE. WHY NOT?

THE BLA-

THOSE SCARY DUDES FROM THE NEWS?

AND IS THIS YOUR RETINUE?

FEE'S WITH ME, YEAH.

JUST A FRIEND. NOT AFFILIATED.

THE OTHER TWO ARE STR PERFORMERS, I BELIE

ONE MOMENT, MISS CHONG.

LOST MY JOB, GOT KIDNAPPED, NOW IT TURNS OUT YOU'RE A MAFIA PRINCESS...

WE ARE NOT THE MAFIA!

ACCESS GRANTED.

PLEASE PROCEED TO THE MAIN HALL WHERE A REPRESENTATIV WILL GREET YOU.

94

WH-WHAT?

NO! NO, THIS WAS...

I SHOULD BE IN THERE!

HEY, Y'KNOW WHAT...?

GUESS MY WISH CAME TRUE!

LOSERRRR!

NOW BE A GOOD LOYAL SOLDIER AND STAND GUARD OUT THERE, YEAH?

LET ME IN!

LET ME IIIIIIIIII-

WHAP

CLANG

... BACK TO THE VILLA, BOSS?

...WHAT EVEN IS THIS PLACE?

BEATS ME... BUT IT LOOKS EXPENSIVE.

AND GIVEN HOW MUCH INFLUENCE PROVIDENCE HAS, IT'S PROBABLY A PLACE FOR SOME PRETTY SERIOUS...

BEHOLD ME

FOR I AM PROVIDENCE

WHAT THE HELL...?

BEHOLD! BEHOLD!

I HAVE PROMISED YOU GROWTH, AND GROWTH YOU SHALL HAVE! UNDER MY LEADERSHIP, WE SHALL SOAR TO NEW HEIGHTS OF –

SHANK

BOOT

BEHOLD ME!

BEHOLD! BEHOL

KLIK KLAK

GAH-!

EXCUSE ME, MISS CHONG?

KLIK KLAK · KLIK KLAK

HELLO, I'M GR-01.

THIS WAY, PLEASE.

I'M REALLY EXCITED TO BE TALKING TO YOU.

BLACK LOTUS ARE ONE OF THE FEW GROUPS IN CASH CITY WE HAVE NO ARRANGEMENTS WITH.

I'D LOVE TO HEAR WHAT A SYNDICATE SPECIALISED IN SHADOW COMMERCE CAN DO FOR US!

WELL... YOU OBVIOUSLY KNOW WHO WE ARE ALREADY.

BUT WE'D LIKE TO KNOW A LITTLE MORE ABOUT PROVIDENCE.

OH, WELL, NOW... WHERE TO BEGIN?

FIRST AND FOREMOST, WE'RE INVESTORS. WE MAKE WEALTH GROW.

WE'VE BEEN AROUND A FEW DECADES, THANKS TO THE OL' BRAIN-CASES.

OUR AIM WAS SIMPLE: FIND OPPORTUNITIES, INVEST IN THEM, AND RE-INVEST THE PROFITS.

TINK TINK

ONCE WE MADE ENOUGH MONEY, PEOPLE DRIFTED TOWARDS US. EVERYONE WANTED A SLICE.

SO WE STARTED USING THEM AS PROXIES. WE ALSO BUILT TWO THINGS TO MAKE OUR LIVES EASIER:

THE PYRAMID.

AND THE TRANSIT NEXUS.

97

YOU...

YOU'RE THE ONES THAT BUILT THE TRANSIT NEXUS?

OH YEAH!

COMPANIES WANTED A DEREGULATED MARKETPLACE TO DO BUSINESS IN. SO WE PROVIDED IT!

OF COURSE, THE DATA WE RECEIVE IS INVALUABLE IN KEEPING US TWO STEPS AHEAD.

WE MONITOR THE MARKETS AND REWARD PROFITABLE PROXIES. WE DON'T EVEN NEED TO INSTRUCT THEM ANYMORE.

THEY HANDLE EVERYTHING FOR US. WE JUST WATCH THE NUMBERS GO UP. EASY!

YOU... LET YOUR PROXIES DO WHATEVER THEY WANT?

WHAT HAPPENS WHEN THEY DO SOMETHING...

I DUNNO, ILLEGAL, OR HARMFUL?

OH, WELL, WE USED TO WORRY ABOUT THAT. WE WERE ALWAYS MONITORING THE NEWSFEEDS.

BUT WHEN WE REALISED A LOT OF THE BAD NEWS WAS DUE TO OUR PROFITABLE INVESTMENTS, WELL...

IT MADE US SAD.

SO WE JUST STOPPED RECEIVING ANYTHING OTHER THAN FINANCIAL DATA.

OH! ONE OF MY INVESTMENTS JUST UPDATED.

EXCUSE ME A SECOND.

PING!

ELLE..?

YOU OKAY?

...OUR CITY IS SECRETLY RUN...

BY IMMORTAL CYBORGS WITH HOARDS OF CASH...

...WHO STOPPED CARING ABOUT PEOPLE BECAUSE IT MADE THEM 'TOO SAD'.

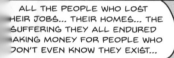

ALL THE PEOPLE WHO LOST THEIR JOBS... THEIR HOMES... THE SUFFERING THEY ALL ENDURED MAKING MONEY FOR PEOPLE WHO DON'T EVEN KNOW THEY EXIST...

I WANNA BURN THIS PLACE TO THE GROUND, FEE.

FOR EVERYONE IN THE CITY. PROVIDENCE. MUST. FALL.

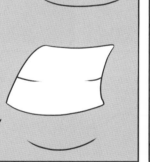

WHERE THE HELL DO WE MAKE A START DOING THAT, THOUGH? THEY'RE SO EMBEDDED IN EVERYTHING!

HUH... Y'KNOW...

SOMETIMES YOU GET A STUBBORN BIKE, YEAH? ONBOARD COMPUTER WON'T LET IT START IF IT DOESN'T GET WHAT IT WANTS.

MAYBE YOU USED A COMPETITOR PART, OR THEY PROGRAMMED IN A SCRAP DATE.

WELL, ME AND UNCLE RAY USED TO FOOL 'EM. RIGGED UP OUR OWN SIGNAL GENERATORS.

IF THEY SEE WHAT THEY EXPECT TO SEE, THEY'LL LET YOU DO WHATEVER. THESE GUYS? THEY'RE NO DIFFERENT.

DUDE! YOU CAN 100% RETAIN YOUR PANTS TOO, I PROMISE!

PLAF
PLAF
PLAF

IF I CAN'T HAVE EVERYTHING...

...I MIGHT AS WELL HAVE **NOTHING.**

NATURE WILL PROVIDE FOR ME IN THE HILLS!

DON'T CARE!

YOU, MASKY. YOU WORK FOR US NOW, RIGHT?

SIGH YES.

GOT A JOB FOR YOU.

TAKE THIS TO THE TRANSIT NEXUS. USE IT TO OVERWRITE THE CORE AI.

...WHAT'S THAT GONNA DO?

REMOVE PROVIDENCE'S INFLUENCE OVER THE CITY'S ECONOMY. GOT A PROBLEM WITH THAT?

...

...WHAT THE HELL. SURE.

JUST KEEP PAYING ME.

WHERE ARE WE GOING?

WE'VE GOT A LOT OF WORK TO DO. C'MON.

FIRST, WE'RE GONNA REPURPOSE BIG GEE'S SERVER FARM.

THE PROGRAM THAT MERC IS INSTALLING WILL FEED US ALL DATA GOING IN AND OUT OF THE TRANSIT NEXUS.

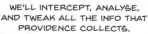

WE'LL INTERCEPT, ANALYSE, AND TWEAK ALL THE INFO THAT PROVIDENCE COLLECTS.

WHAT ARE WE GONNA DO WITH ALL THE DATA?

≶SNRK≷ I AUTOMATED AN OFF-THE-SHELF TAX PROGRAM.

THE NEXUS WILL CALCULATE AND PAY THE TAXES EACH COMPANY SHOULD BE PAYING...

PLUS A LITTLE EXTRA FROM PROVIDENCE.

AND WHAT ABOUT PROVIDENCE?

THEY'LL LIVE IN BLISSFUL IGNORANCE, WATCHING FAKE NUMBERS GO UP.

... AND ALL OF THIS IS GONNA WORK? RIGHT?

...GOD, I HOPE SO.

ONLY TIME WILL TELL.

...SHUTTERING THEIR OPERATIONS IN CASH CITY, ADDING TO THE RECENT WAVE OF UNEMPLOYMENT.

MANY CORPORATIONS, PARTICULARLY THOSE WHOSE STOCK PRICES HAVE YET TO RECOVER, HAVE DECLARED THE EVENT A 'DISASTER'.

BUT HAS THE CRASH BEEN ALL BAD?

OF COURSE, NOBODY WANTS ANYONE TO LOSE THEIR JOB, AND IT'S DISAPPOINTING THAT SO FEW COMPANIES HAVE DONE RIGHT BY THEIR WORKERS.

BUT WITH COMPANIES NOW PAYING TAX AS THEY SHOULD, WE'VE BEEN ABLE TO IMPROVE OUR SOCIAL SECURITY PROGRAMS.

SUBSISTENCE ALLOWANCES, EDUCATION, LEGAL AID... THEY'VE ALL SOFTENED THE BLOW SUBSTANTIALLY.

CSN | Tracy Martinez, Bayside Ward Councillor

IN FACT, WE'RE STARTING TO SEE NEW BUSINESSES AND WORKER CO-OPS FORMING.

HEY, BOSS.

AND WE LOOK FORWARD TO SUPPORTING THEM!

NEXT:

NEW REPORTS CAME IN.

THANKS, X.

LOOKS LIKE THINGS MIGHT REALLY BE HEADING TOWARDS STABILITY.

OH, THANK GOD.

MAYBE WE CAN FINALLY STOP STRESSING ABOUT IT, NOW.

EH. THERE'LL ALWAYS BE SOMETHING TO BE STRESSED ABOUT. AT LEAST EVERYONE'S ON A MORE EVEN FOOTING THAN BEFORE.

EVEN IF WE HAD TO, UH... KINDA DESTROY SOCIETY TO DO IT.

...HOW LONG DO YOU RECKON IT'LL LAST?

TCH. WHO KNOWS?

THERE'LL BE ANOTHER PROVIDENCE SOMEWHERE ALONG THE LINE, NO DOUBT.

BUT MAYBE PEOPLE HAVE WHAT THEY NEED TO STAND UP TO THEM, NOW.

SO...

ARE YOU REALLY HEADING OUT? YOU CAN TOTALLY STAY HERE, Y'KNOW...

THANKS, ELLE. FOR ALL OF THIS. BUT RIGHT NOW... I JUST WANNA GET BACK TO NORMAL. BESIDES... BAYSIDE BURGER CO-OP! WHO'DA THOUGHT IT?

HOW 'BOUT YOU? WHAT'LL YOU DO?

DUNNO YET. I KINDA LIKE THIS WHOLE ROBIN HOOD DEAL. MAYBE CASH CITY NEEDS A FRIEND IN THE SHADOWS...?

EH, YOU'LL FIGURE IT OUT. BUT I PROMISE YOU -

- YOU'LL NEVER FACE A CRISIS ALONE.

HELL YEAH!

CLINK!

NEWT SODA

END

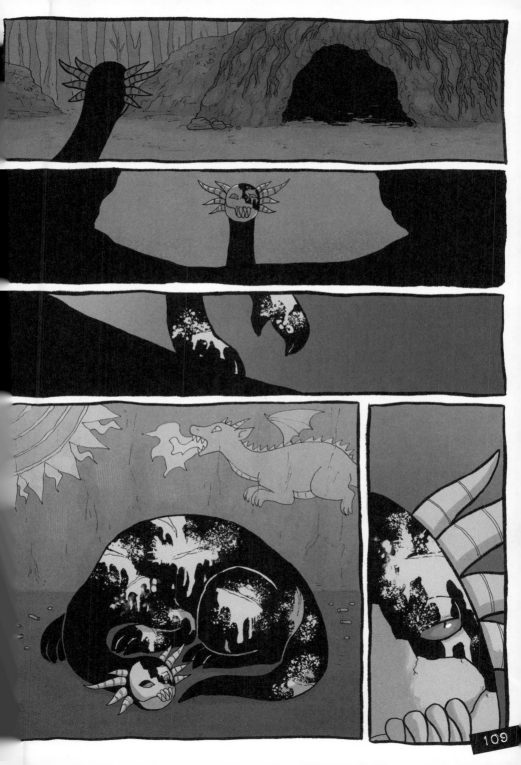

AH, I'M SORRY I SCARED YOU! I'M NOT GONNA HURT YOU, HONEST! THIS PLACE IS USUALLY MY DEN, YOU SEE..

I CAME DOWN HERE TO PLAY AND I SAW YOU! AND YOU LOOK REAL HURT, SO I WANTED TO CHECK ON YOU.

I'LL GO GET SOME STUFF THAT CAN HELP YOU!

DON'T GO ANYWHERE, I'LL BE RIGHT BACK!

111

OH GOOD, YOU'RE STILL HERE!

I FIGURED YOU'D BE HUNGRY, SO I BROUGHT THE BEST SNACK IN THE WORLD...

CHEESE AND JAM SANDWICHES!

IF YOU'RE NOT HUNGRY, THAT'S OKAY.

I'LL LEAVE IT HERE FOR YOU.

MY NAME'S TRAN!

I'M NINE YEARS OLD AND MY FAVOURITE COLOUR'S YELLOW.

I LIKE STRAWBERRIES, DRAWING, READING...

YOU KNOW I'VE NEVER SEEN ANYTHING LIKE YOU BEFORE.

BUT YOU HAD TO HAVE COME FROM SOMEWHERE, RIGHT?

DO YOU HAVE ANY FAMILY?

I'M SORRY...
I DIDN'T MEAN TO
UPSET YOU.

I DON'T KNOW
WHAT HAPPENED
BEFORE...

BUT NOW
THAT WE'RE FRIENDS I
PROMISE I'M NOT GONNA
LEAVE YOU, OKAY?

UH, HI. SORRY I HAVEN'T BEEN BY FOR A FEW DAYS.

THINGS HAVE BEEN BUSY... AT HOME.

DADDY'S CROPS DID BADLY...

I TRIED TO BE GOOD...

I REALLY, REALLY TRIED...

B—BUT I WAS SO SCARED OF UPSETTING DADDY THAT I KNOCKED THE SOUP OVER...

THE END

THE LAST STOP

BY LIO PRESSLAND

HEY MORAG, NEED ANY HELP?

GOT IT!

WE'RE GOOD, THANK YOU, CALEB.

THERE'S SOME FOOD ON THE SIDE FOR YOU.

FOUND THE WHISK. TRICKY LIL FELLA.

OH, YOU DIDN'T HAVE TO DO THAT.

TAKE YOUR TIME TO EAT IT, TOO.

THE TRAIN WON'T BE HERE FOR ANOTHER WEE WHILE, AND KELSEY CAN FINISH THE REST OF THE CLEANING.

NO, NO, I CAN JUST—

CALEB.

OKAY, OKAY, SORRY!

THANK YOU FOR THE SANDWICH.

REMEMBER TO *CHEW* THIS TIME!

OH, THAT LOOKS TASTY! LOOK, WE'RE ALL DONE, SO YOU CAN RELAX.

YEAH, I'VE ALREADY BEEN TOLD OFF BY THE OTHER TWO.

YOU DON'T HAVE TO HELP EVERYONE, CALEB.

BUT THAT'S WHAT-

THAT'S WHAT THE CAFE IS FOR, I KNOW.

BUT IT DOESN'T HAVE TO ALL BE UP TO YOU.

AHH?!?

TRAIN'S EARLY!

HUH? THAT'S WEIRD.

GUYS! ...AIN'S HERE!!

WHAT?! WHEN HAS THE TRAIN EVER BEEN EARLY?! *AAAHHHH!!*

OH MY GODS, I NEED TO PUT THE CAKE IN THE OVEN *NOW!*

HELLO, GOOD MORNING, WELCOME TO THE LAST STOP!

OPEN

CLACK

CLOSED

PHEW, THAT WAS A LONG DAY, HUH?

COULD YOU BRING IN THE SIGN?

OH YES, OF COURSE, NO PROBLEM!

EXCUSE ME? UM...

I DON'T KNOW WHICH TRAIN I'M SUPPOSED TO GET ON.

HEY GUYS...

UM...

MEET KIP...

THE HUMAN.

PFFFT

THANK YOU FOR THE COFFEE.

OF COURSE.

SO... KIP, WAS IT?

HOW DID YOU GET HERE?

WERE YOU TRICKED? LURED?

FELL INTO A PORTAL?

HE MUST BE A DEMON OF SOME KIND.

WEIR
LOOK
DEMO

I'M NOT A DEMON.

ALL I REMEMBER IS...

I DIED.

I WOKE UP ON A TRAIN AND WAS GIVEN A BLANK TICKET.

I GOT OFF HERE, THE NONE OF THE OT TRAINS WOULD ME ON.

I WAS TOO NERVOUS TO COME IN HERE AND ASK WHAT WAS GOING ON.

ARE YOU GUYS NOT GODS?

OH, NO, WE'VE BARELY EVEN SEEN THE GODS!

WE'RE MOSTLY LESSER SPIRITS.

KELSEY IS A KELPIE, MORAG IS A STANDING STONE, HARRIS IS A HAGGIS, AND I'M...

OR, WELL, I WAS A GUARDIAN OF A TREE.

"WAS"?

I-

HEY, SO, UH...

WHAT DID THEY SAY?

THEY SAID HE'LL BE GONE BY MORNING.

WHAT?!

HE'S NOT A SPIRIT, HE CAN'T STAY IN THE SPIRIT REALM.

HIS BODY IS JUST GOING TO START DISAPPEARING.

THERE'S NOTHING WE CAN DO.

NO...

WE CAN'T LET THAT HAPPEN, HE- HE COULD GET ON ONE OF THE TRAINS AN-

CALEB. HE DIDN'T EVEN GET A PROPER TICKET.

THAT MEANS THERE ISN'T ANYWHERE FOR HIM TO GO.

I SAID I'D HELP HIM.

134

DO YOU WANT TO KNOW WHY I MADE THIS CAFE?

HM?

I MADE IT SO THAT WHEREVER THE DEAD GO FOR THEIR AFTERLIFE, THEY CAN HAVE SOME PEACE ON THEIR JOURNEY.

THEY CAN HAVE A COFFEE, A LITTLE SOMETHING TO EAT, AND PONDER THEIR LIFE. THEY CAN FINISH THEIR LAST PAINTING, FINISH THAT BOOK THEY'VE BEEN MEANING TO GET AROUND TO...

A PLACE OF PEACE AND COMFORT THAT SOME PEOPLE MAY NEVER HAVE GOTTEN TO EXPERIENCE.

I MADE IT FOR THE GHOSTS WHO PASS THROUGH, BUT ALSO FOR SPIRITS WHO HAVE LOST THEIR PURPOSE.

SOME LOST THEIR WAY BECAUSE PEOPLE STOPPED BELIEVING IN THEM...

SOME LOST THEIR HOME TO DESTRUCTION OR TIME.

WE ALL NEED A PLACE TO FEEL SAFE, TO FEEL NEEDED.

YOU SAID YOU WERE A GUARDIAN OF A TREE?

YEAH...

I WAS.

OH MY GODS. ESALE IS HERE.

SHE'S THE ONE WE NEED TO TALK TO? THE GOD OF THE SPIRIT REALM, RIGHT?

THAT'S HER. ARE YOU READY?

I THINK SO...

WE HAVE THE OFFERING.

WE HEARD SHE LIKES SWISS ROLLS, SO FINGERS CROSSED!

SHE'S OUTSIDE.

LET'S DO THIS. I'M HERE.

THE END

149

JULIE CAMPBELL

BY THE WAY (PG. 1)

A comic creator and wildlife/landscape illustrator living in Fife.

campbelldraws.com

 @JCampbelldraws @juliecampbelldraws

JACK DEVEREAUX

GASTROTELEPATHY (PG. 27)

A comic creator based in Worcester, whose comics have been described by his mum as "yes, okay, dear".

jackdevereaux.com

 @Deverfro @clouddevereaux

CARA GAFFNEY

IN LILAC & SILVER (PG. 53)

A comic artist and writer from Glasgow, creator of the webcomic *Fault Lines* and SICBA-nominated fantasy comic *Wellheart*.

caragaffney.com

 @AriadneArca @AriadneArca

CHRIS MANSON

F! PROVIDENCE (PG. 81)

A mixed Cantonese-Scottish comic creator based in Glasgow makes speculative fiction exploring issues of identity and challenging traditionalism.

chrislaumanson.co.uk

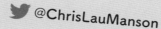 @ChrisLauManson   @ChrisLauManson

DOMINIQUE DUONG

THE MONSTER & THE GIRL (PG. 107)

An illustrator and comic artist based in London, who seeks to create diverse, queer fantasy and horror stories. Has a love for surreal, conceptual imagery.

domduong.com

 @domduongart   @domgduongart

LIO PRESSLAND

THE LAST STOP (PG. 125)

A transmasc nonbinary comic artist and illustrator from Scotland.

kroov.club

 @kroovv

BEHIND

THE SCENES

WRITING THE SCRIPT

PAGE 9

1|2
344
344

<u>PANEL 1</u>
She pinches her nose, trying to
pull herself together.

<u>PANEL 2</u>
Arina half-rises from the bench.
Arina: Can I hug you?

<u>PANEL 3</u>
Cleo nods wordlessly.

<u>PANEL 4</u>
Arina pulls her in.

Page 12
Panel 1

Upper left of page. The closest, most detailed
look we've gotten of The Pyramid against the
night sky and skyline. It is a tall, imposing
structure that appears to be constructed from
dark reflective glass, not unlike the Louvre.
Piping and cables occasionally erupt from it,
only to disappear back into the building.

Panel 2

Upper right of page. Long shot as BIG GEE's car
screeches to a halt in a city street at the base of
the Pyramid, which has a footprint the size of a
large office building. A large rectangular recess is
built into the front of it, that seems to be the sole
entryway into the structure. A few scattered
passers-by watch on in mild indifference. BIG
GEE is already trying to step out of the car door,
even though the vehicle is still moving.
SFX:
Screeeeeeeech!

STEP #2

THUMBNAILING

WARRIOR
THINGS

STEP #3

PENCILLING

STEP #4

INKING

STEP #5

ADD GREYSCALE AND TEXT, AND YOU'RE DONE!

MORE FROM
QUINDRIE PRESS

The Beechwood Helm
by Letty Wilson

Returning home from battle, two knights come upon a strange figure in red armour, who challenges them to a fight to the death.

Answering the challenge invites a terrible curse, which only love can break.

"It's bloody beautiful in every way."
- Joe Thompson, Comic Book News UK

The Nightingale and the Rose
by Jem Milton

In a remote magical college, a student pines after their beautiful potions partner.

Hoping to help the student capture her heart, a nightingale who believes in true love begins a journey to find them a red rose to complete the spell.

But the only way to conjure a red rose is to pay a terrible price...

What the Witch Saw
by Thomas Heitler

The United Nations sends a team of Witches to terraform the Moon into a world lush with life.

Even though they're working for a brighter future, one Witch finds herself struggling with her past.

It all starts with a Seed...

Wolvendaughter by Ver

Bent on destruction, the Beast cuts a swathe through towns and countryside, accompanied by its lone herald, the Daughter. A fable about the cycle of ruin and rebirth, perseverance, duty, and a grim hope.

"The work of an undeniable major newer talent."
 - Andy Oliver, Broken Frontier

Nominated for the Eisner Award for Best Single Issue/One-Shot 2022

Recoil Book 1: Flood by Spire Eaton

After causing a fatal accident, Kalo is kidnapped into superpower therapy. But something doesn't feel right about the Croft Centre for the Attributed. He's struggling with his guilt, losing time, and soon a dark secret comes to light...

"[Recoil] feels like a slickly produced work that you'd expect to see coming out of a major publisher, so to learn that it was created by a single person isn't just impressive, it's astonishing."
 - Amy Walker, Set The Tape

When I Was Me: Moments of Gender Euphoria edited by Eve Greenwood & Alex Assan

A collection of autobiographical comics about the joyful experiences of being transgender. Featuring comics and illustrations from over 70 worldwide contributors.

"Groundbreaking."
 - Maggie Baska, Pink News

Winner of the Broken Frontier Award for Best One-Shot Anthology 2021

QUINDRIE PRESS

Quindrie Press
is an independent comics
publisher based in Edinburgh, Scotland.
Our focus is to provide creators with the
opportunity to publish passion project
comics that haven't found their home
anywhere else.

FIND MORE COMICS AT QUINDRIEPRESS.COM

EVE GREENWOOD

A nonbinary comic
creator, letterer, and editor
who spends way too much
time thinking about languages.
Makes the award-nominated
webcomic *Inhibit*.

evegwood.com

 @evegwood

HARI CONNER

Hari is a transmasc
fantasy dweeb and hopeless
forest romantic. Read their
award-winning webcomic
Finding Home or learn more
about their other books
at their website.

hari-illustration.com

 @haridraws